ABS
BEYOND VIZION

By Ricardo A. Owens

© 2010 Mynd Entertainment
All Rights Reserved

No part of this book may be reproduced, stored in a retrieval system, or transmitted by any means without the written permission of the author.

Published By:
Vision Distribution, LLC.
Nine Music Square South, Suite 407
Nashville, TN (615) 296-0960
www.visiondistribution.com
Printed in the USA

Poetry beyond the vizion of thought, abstract to the mind

In "Abstract Beyond Vizion" many expressions are of myself (Ricardo A. Owens), and expressions of life, love, and, its struggles, etc. This book of poetry was written based on ones self experiences and personal views of things through life being lived.

Growing up as a child having a brain tumor at the age of (4yrs. old), a stroke during surgery, taking physical therapy until the age of (16yrs. old). Through all of this, being left partially paralyzed for the rest of my life, experiencing two more strokes at the ages of (19 & 23yrs old).

Through these experiences and life changes, struggle was endured. But from these things, being tried, despised, and, criticized strength was brought to life, that you the reader will encounter multiple times over. As life is lived more strength is obtained, which this strength obtained is shared in the form of motivation, inspiring that drive of ambition to do what is denied many.

ABOUT THE AUTHOR

Ricardo A. Owens
AKA

"Sohlja" tha poet

Over all, this book is written to be an inspiration to its world of readers. By being told something is impossible for you. "Do It" and "Do It" Better than your expected Too!!!

ABOUT CONTENT

Attention!!!

All content in this book of many pages, does not contain proper English & spelling throughout it's entirety. This book of poetry has been designed to benefit more than one audience of viewers in different ways.

TABLE OF CONTENTS

(Introduction)

Seduced	9

(Section I)

Poemi (Poetry of Me)	10
The Soul of <u>This</u> Blackman	11
Get to know me	13
Blind	14
Tears in my Mind	15
Chain Links	16
The Tint of my Skinn	17
In My Thinking Box	18
Soul Motivation	19
Circuit Overload	20
Deep, the Unexperienced side "of me"	21
Life	22
That "shoulder" to cry on	23
Frustrated	24
Releasin me	25
The life of Me	26
Aggression under Fire	28
Addiktion	29
The Deception of Doubt	30
Matrimony	31
Can I	32
Under Estimate	34
Ambition	36
Humility	37
Crafted & Ingraved	38

(Section II)

Luv'oetry (Love Poetry)	39
Love	40
Rejoiced	41
Love is	42
Attractive	43
Have you Ever	44
Ephiktion	45
Expressions	46
Wrong Observation	47
Sexxi	48
Iz it worth it	50
My Desire	51
So Sad	52
Lately Its Been You	53
So many things (All about you)	54
A Love so Passionate	55
My Mind	56
Into You	57
Loves Letter	58
Luv Joy	60
Makin Luv	61
Unique Beauti	62

(Section III)

Ghytt'oetry (Ghetto Poetry)	64
Incarcerated	65
On the Edge	66
Reverse Psychology	67
Fam	68
Real	69
Poetry of the Street	70
Thugg Motif	71
Juvenile Mind	72
Listen to the Crys	73
Unity	74
Ghytto Ethycks	75
Imitation	76
Kon'tamenated	77
Locked	78
Revoked	79
Affiliated	81
Rebel Rebeller	83
Spent	84
Walkin with Shame	86
Spot Lyte	87
A Childs Ghytto Story	88

(Section IV)

Lyfe'oetry (Life Poetry)	90
This Life	91
Life-N-Brail	92
The Antichrist	93
M'phasize	94
Experience	95
Sentenced 2 Death	96
When We Don't Understand	97
Tyr'd Soul	98
Diamonds in the Ruff	99
Graffiti Walls	100
Soul Veins	101
The Rendering	102
Drunk	103
What Do You Think	104
Help Needed	105
When Things Ain't Right	106
Lookin Past the Darkness	107
Sold	108
To Be Deceived	109
Self Affliction	110
Tapped	111
Self Xamination	112
Feel The Vibes	113
Raped	114
Naked	116
Slow Motion	117
Thru Tha Rain	118
Luv Jones	119
Xistance	120
Seasoned	122

Seduced

Let me be your
crack & cocaine
get inside your mind
stimulate your brain,
your medical marijuana
and ease your pain,
your alcohol
changing the direction
of your thoughts train
Painting a portrait
not seen visually
but with words verbally

Let me seduce you poetically
let me undress your mind
xposin the unknown on the outside
have your interest confided
to that something
on the outside

Can I jog your mind
like the unfamiliar taste
of new food being tried,
enjoying that savory
taste obtained,
indulgin more into
that which was once strange
verbally
vocally
& mentally,
Through these words of poetry
you will be
"seduced"

Poemi
(Poetry of Me)

Expressions of myself
&
opinions of thought about things,
experiences of my life

-The Soul of <u>this</u> Blackman
-Get to know me
-Blind
-Tears in my mind
-Chain Links
-The tint of my skinn
-Soul Motivation
-Circuit Overload
-Deep, the unexperienced side "of me"
-Life
-That "shoulder" to cry on
-Frustrated
-Releasin me
-The life of me
-Aggression under fire
-Addiktion
-The deception of doubt
-Matrimony
-Can I
-Ambition
-Humility
-Crafted & Ingraved
-What do you think
-In my thinking box
-Under estimate
- When things aint right

The "Soul" of "<u>This</u>" "Blackman"

Humble & meek
pushed to the peek
tested to reach the point of weak,
So instead of grittin my teeth and frown
I laugh about it and smile
Instead of unfold and loose control
I stay fold'ed, and maintain a firm hold of my control on;
The "Soul" of "<u>this</u>" "Blackman"

Instead of takin from the less fortunate,
I "would" rather give and receive nothing back in return
but to earn and collect respect,
Yet instead of my kindness takin for it's positiveness
it's takin for a weakness an unfilled bleakness

The "Soul" of "<u>this</u>" "Blackman"
In a world so cruel
his heart seem so cold,
because it's not a possession that
the world is allowed to grasp and hold,
because of this soul
this Blackman is in control,

The "Soul" of "<u>this</u>" "Blackman"

Cold from rejection
is kept warm by ambition
motivated by those that hate its being,

Cause to it
that hate it can't relate
so it tryz to debate
what it cant make or break,
tryin to prohibit and hesitate the decision that
won't be stopped
from being made within
The "Soul" of "<u>this</u>" "Blackman"

An urged expressin feelin
from the bowels of the heart,
Burnin like a forrest fire out of control
With an overwhelming joyous expression of
accomplishment

The "Soul" of "<u>this</u>" "Blackman"
Dark like a dungeon to the world
kept private like someone to their self
or the deepest of kept secrets,
With alms of confidentiality
silent like an empty room with no existence
is how the world seez this Blackman
Get know me beyond what you see
get to know me through poetry
as The "Soul" of "<u>this</u>" "Blackman" live free

Get to know me

You think you know me
but don't know me
your so blind
you don't realize when your lookin at me
you see my appearance
not my ways of life,
my ways of right
I'm a simple man
that you don't understand
a Godly man that the world don't care to
be friend
and you say you know me
but don't know the first thing about me
you only know what the hear
but what you see is that,
I'm complicated like a combination
hard to understand,
you can throw dirt on me
I'm still gonna shine,
lettin the rain from the storm wash
the dirt from my back
and sand from my eyez
makin me shine so bright
that it leavez you blind

"Get to know me"

Blind

Everyday in this life is a day in the battlefield
I can get wounded in war,
and still heal
"get" shot down by the evil of the world
and not get killed
yet,
just a simple man that the world don't
"understand"
"striv'in" to "be" a Godly man that the world
care not to understand
with ways
deep'er than the o'cean
wider than the s'ea;

some people that say they know me
"but" they don't know me,
they only know what they hear
and "what" they are
told about me

with a combination so complicated
I'm "hard" to break in,

throw dirt on me still I'm going to shine,

I'm gonna let the gleam from the shine,
take the grime from my life
and still shine "so bright"
that you gonna be blinded

Tears in my Mind

Tears in my mind,
cause my emotionz
want lets them come,
from my eyez,
So I feel the
pain and hurt inside
cryin without wet eyes
"with"
Tears in my mind
Wounded,
swold up and dying
bleedin internally
what
you can't see of me

Fat from sorrow
is this soul
from it's crys

leavin
Tears in my mind
instead of water as
tears in my eyes

Chain Links

The links of struggle that lead to lengthens of success
the road to accomplishments,
leaving more space for achievement
establish prosperity from progress;
Like chainz on tires in the ice & snow,
struggle make me strong so
I can make it through the muck & mire that the world leadz me too,
see me struggle watch me fail,
that's what the world wantz to do;

The links of struggle that leads to strength
like weight on my shoulder it hangz around my neck,
Like the link of struggle worn as a belt
I wear it around my waist not only my neck,
with a big belt buckle that sayz "Sohlja"
cause the struggle I'm survivin it
Chain Links

like unity each link equals strength,
Like accomplishin a goal,
Equaling achievement
So does the links of a chain together, equal strength

The Tint of My Skinn

On my flesh it wears thick
causing the success of my prosperity
to run thin,
Causing ambition to thrive,
not to descend to an end
allowing the experience of things
that many say;
has no business being

"The tint of my Skinn"
Something that glow like the gliss of gold,
something for life;
that I will forever cherish and hold,
as Samsons hair was his strength
mine is my tint
the many shades of brown
considered to as black

"The tint of my Skinn"
does many it
"attract"

In My Thinkin Box

It don't got to be any special place
I can be in it any time
any place
any where,
don't even got to have a chair
to sit in,
like a flash of light I can be in that box
havin thoughts that flow like a river while
I'm in it
It's like bein in a state of concentration
that can't be broken,
a train of thought in which thinking
is intensely deep

In my thinking box
is where I be

Soul Motivation

Touching you deeper than sexual affections
stronger than the tides of the ocean in a fast
moving motion,

Touching you deep within
down to the roots where bowels begin
having the moving impact like strong emotion,

Infecting the inter realm of the non'esteemed being
inspiring that being to go beyond their means,

Erupting like a volcano
effecting the environment in which it exist
with what never existed before;
evolving into the presence of that which has always
been in place
that was never before seen,

Presently becoming into existence is ambition
the drive, to go forth with what you're scared to
approach because you didn't know it

Soul Motivation
hidden existing ambition
of the enter being
drivin by another inspiration

Circuit Overload

Tired of being sick and tired
by the world tired of bein tried
like my wires are crossed
I got a Circuit Overload
and I'm ready to just burn or explode,

Its like at times I don't know what to do
but I do what I know how too
the rest I let do
and me bein me like you being you
it's like burden on my back
agony screamz from my mind,

"causin" my strength like my back
that's broken from burden
beginz to get weak
because of the oppression
that tend to be experienced but not seeked
therefore leavin me bleak,

Leavin me on journey for shelter to shield me
from the cold of the world to which I'm exposed
causing my circiut to overload
setting me on fire
from the crossing of my wires
blowin a fuse becomin bad news

Deep,
The Unexperienced Side of Me

Deep like the water that make the sea
so deep to the point that you can't see me
deep beyond the depts of visually
deep like it's bottom
which from it's top you can't see
cloudy like muddy water
confusin like an elusion;

Like an unsolved mystery of history
is the intensity of it's existing
it's being,
that being foreseen
by the nonunderstanding being

Deep like valleys low
like exploring places never journeyed before
leaving much to obtain
deep like a sunken ship, with "a" hidden treasure,

Deep
is the worlds unexperienced
side of me

Life

The good, the bad
The strength, the weakness

The joy, the pain
The sunshine, the rain

Things we gain
Some we can't maintain

The struggle, the strain
The stress on the brain

Tryin to maintain
From which is hard to sustain

With Satan in the veins
Like a derailed train

When all you cry is tears of pain
Like water from a drain
Sweat from frustration pours from the lock of hair
on the head
Like water from standin in the rain

And still there's no relief from the pain
As it pours like water from the rain

It's "Life"

"That shoulder to cry on"

Not a shoulder to shed tears on
that shoulder similar to an ear
someone to hear that reality of me
see the pain
that I feel
when thing change from beauty to ugly,
"yet" still be there
through the cryz of anguish, the pain, the struggle
the strain to maintain

"That shoulder to cry on"
Listen to the cryz from inside
that can't be seen, but hidden
someone that's going to ride it out like a Bahama
cruise
in it for the long ride
someone that's going to be
there
that motivation to be strong
and move on

Many days I cry in many ways
but not one day doez water run down my face
through pain I cry, through struggle I cry
devastatin frustration,
life with a twisted
confused people

Sometimez, someone is needed just to be there

That ear to hear
"That shoulder to cry on"

Frustrated

As I sit and stare
In the air's a glare
A glance at life and what's
not there

an empty space
a blain face
as if somethingzs out of order
and not in place

from the blain
to the bleak
passed the depression
the coldness
it's relief that's seeked

Releasin Me

Can I express me
Can I be real, like life & death
Can I be sudden, like the releasing of held breath
Can I give you my all, like it's the last I got left

Can I get to know you, and you know me
before you say no, give me a chance
"please"
cause you, really don't know me
all you "might" know is that I'm good peeps
but deep down inside you really don't know me
that's the side of you that I would like to reach
"deep"
can I undress your mind and see your insides
like a nude body
can I see your real side

Can I be me
can I set myself free
like a bundle of stress released up off of me
can I be me, by speakin lyrically or poetically
can I be unique and just be

My ways are deeper than the ocean
spreaded wider than the sea
so complex a palm reader can't read me
unmagnifyable;
through a magnifying glass
you can't magnify me

The life of Me

Sometime it's amazing
sometime it's amusing
the positive things I do
"people" it's not fazing
but their wrath is hot at my trail
and blazin
like hot metal to the skin
to my soul is brazin
sendin me in a spiral through
so many changes & fazes
with their wrath hot on my trail and blazin
like Satans fiery from hell
like hot metal to the skin
my soul is blazin
sendin me in a spiral through so many
changes & fazes
to the point that it feel normal
not like anything new or meeting
strangers
to me livin in torment is nothing new
it seemz to feel like some'thin normal to do
My life is hell
My life is hate
to the things in my life some people
can't relate
sometimez I ask myself
how do I make it
it's like I give myself to the world
and my life it tryz to take
receivin nothin back
my heart getz cold and turnz black
because into a thousand pieces

it's already cracked,

sometimez "I wish" I could take it all back
and be on the receiving end of the track,
but The Life of Me
is complicated like that

The Life of Me
is just that

Aggression under Fire

Pushed to the point of anger
like red hot metal under fire
heated to the point of it's weakness
maintaining its elements of meekness;

Allowing you to obtain affliction in the form of
humility
Becoming humbled,
having the boundary of your comfort zone stepped
beyond
like metal taking on an unexpected
shape
Testing the character of your being
to find your breaking point of meekness
establishing the humbleness of a situation
the point to which it can be pushed
under extreme anger like

Aggression under Fire

Addiktion

Let me be
your cocaine, your caffeine, & nicotine,
all of the above and in between
Let me
Show you what good really is
what love really meanz;
Let me be
that needle in your armz
that sendz a numbness through your veinz

Let me; be
that stimulant to your brain

Let me be
your high when your feelin down
to relax your brain

Let me
have you hooked on my love
like alcohol & crack cocaine

Let me be
the stimulant to which your mind & body relax

Let me be that drug
Let me be that bad habit
Let me be that;
Addiktion;
and have you hooked

The Deception of Doubt

Doubted by the ones you are good too!
because you take action a little differently
than usual

they structure a storage of disbelief, mischief
and, deceit
still from you like a criminal of the night
known as a thief

Tending to set forth a deception
the lead in a direction other than the one taken
from the beginning
when the good things once received
begin to come to an end

Matrimony

Being part of a world that we all must live in
but at the same time having ways that seem to be
different
instead of living according to the ways of the world
you live by your own rules & regulations
like an animal in it's own habitat
living by it's own culture
living by it's own mannerism

Understood by few
misunderstood by many
set out to be misguided and mislead
but proceed to make your own way instead of
following
the misleading
as with my journey I'm proceeding
obtaining strength from those against my being

Criticized
unjustified living in a world
expected to commit suicide
married into a state which can't be escaped

Matrimony

Can I

Can I be free to release me
be, who I be
not how society or the world wantz me to be
is that, ok
is it ok that I do things uniquely
in ways that things are not understood
or seen
by the world or society because I'm
me;

Can I
dress nice and have things
not be rich or have it like some people do;
but struggle to get
what I do

Can I
have trialz & tribulationz
obtain strength instead of devastation
seekin the positive out of negative
and the negative in a positive,
seein between a line that'z so fine
finer than lovez line
deeper than a relationship in which love'z
combined;

Can I
get between that line
deep in your mind like words undefined

like unanswered questions in lifes past
it's behind

Can I
be real
like the feel of cold chills
tell you the truth
about how things really is
life and how "cold" it's people is,
with ways like snake venom
making you cautious to listen
for the sound of vipers hissin,
deadly like a bullet
fired off by a hairpin trigger
once you pull it

Under Estimate

If you could see
inside my mind
there's a line so fine
that can't be defined,
to which you can't relate
between
love & hate
because love I do
2 "hate" I can't relate
2 it I don't hold no appointments
and
don't make no dates
although to love I do
but be picky to choose
that which I except,
keepin the mind sharp like
a razor blade and well equip
like a gun on the hip
prepared for those who attempt
to be swift
as if my blade is dull
and I'm not equip
yet cut deep
and shoot hollow tips
wit my mind
as it's chamber rotatez
and like bullets it spitz
at you
wit words of
knowledge & wisdom

I spit and hit
cutting deeper than a razor
blade
spillin my words
then your gutts,
inflictin the mind inside,
when it's on me that many things
were & are
tried
as my blade I sharpen
and
my chamber revolves
concealin cartridges wit
more impact
inside

Ambition

Like rose pedals to a rose
"throughout" its pedals it gleamz

Like a hummingbird throughout it's wings
Through poetry my heart singz

Like the unique coloring to a butterfliez wingz
It's like beauty to the sky,

from the stars twinkling
like the sun
water & soil
working together
makin something grow;
from a seed to something beautiful,
is lifes positive dwelling

"beautiful", sweet & charming
as a smile on a face
not knowing what it meanz
warming a heart,
filling an empty place
is a reality in a different way
like loving something or someone
in our own way
no matter what people or,
the world got to say
doin what you want anyway
and be;
Be ambitious
"Havin ambition"

Humility

Oh what a friend
is there in it

Humilty
bringz out the best in me
makes me strong
where I'm weak

maken me humble
testin my meek

To me
its been the friend
like an enemy
not a day do I miss
to see
Humility

like the bright sun rayz
that start off the day

Humility
the voice that refusez
not to be heard

That something tryin to make sure
that everything goes the wrong way

Attention in life
unjoyfully
"is"
Humility

Crafted & Ingraved

Through the struggle,
the strain
the loss &
less gain,
the strive to maintain
molded
shaped
Made
into a man
to with stand
the effects from the storm
the strong wind & rain
in the form of
tragedy & pain
through devastation
make it,
the losses
with humble & meekness
take them,
content
in the process
of the things
possessed,
blessed
knowing how to obtain
less stressed
in the process of being
"Crafted & Ingraved"

Who I am
a man

Love'oetry
(love poetry)

Something for the lovers
the husbands, wives
and many relations in this life
that's obtained Love

-Rejoiced
-Love is
-Attractive
-Have you Ever
-Ephiktion
-Expressions
-Wrong Observation
-Sexxi
-Iz it worth it
-My Desire
-So sad
-Lately Its Been You
-The Beauti of Love
-So many thing
All about you
-A Love so Passionate
-My Mind
-Into you
-Loves Letter
-Luv Joy
-Makin Luv
-Unique Beauti

Love

It's nothing to be afraid of,
but wantz you to except it
like it excepts you,
Love, it wants you to except it like it lovez you
the same way it shows its self to you
its not necessarily wanting you to
show yourself to it
but love it back;
It's a wonderful thing to be loved
and have love in your life
a wonderful thing is love, to give to those
who don't get it
Love is a wonderful thing to give to those
Who do get it
but not from everyone

Love can be romantic
touchin you deeper than sex do,
makin you happy when you don't
expect it too
showering you with the presence
of it's strong essence;

Love can be humble
Love can be meek
Love can be in so many ways unique
like the elegance of a physique from its,
curves to its creases like a puzzle of many pieces
put together to make one
from that one comez beauty & strength
in the form of;
Love

Rejoiced

Enjoyed is
The elegant essence
Of your presence,
Like the radiance
Of the sun
melting the snow,
Only you glow
Like the midnight Moon,
Like the lighting of a dark room
so does that essence
to this dark soul
gradually warming
from being cold,
"given" a new shine
to that which was
once dull
and old,
given a positive
sense
of
e-static
joyously
e-radic
the presence of
the suns
warmness
and that glow
of your
midnight moon
that
now is
obtained

Love is

Love is the element of life
that's strong as death
like the taken of a last breath
it's here, that love could be;

But who'z to say;
when the chance hasn't been given to see,
what's beyond a fantasy

Love is like chemistry
a combination of mystery
between two makin one
like the dawn of the moon
to the rayz of the sun
even as they take transition their still one
as they shine abroad the land,
shared throughout the world and all it's nations;
is that love
that comes from up above
the heavenly love

Love is
the creator of the moon
the creator of the sun
that love that makes the world one

Attractive

That something
your attracted too
is what,
the mind
&
it's intelligence
or
is that
"erallivent"
is it that positive vibe
from within the soul,
is it
that sexxi fazique
the average eye seek
"that"
makes the mind peak
that "you"
are attracted too,
to "them"
so attracted are you,
got you wrapped
like the strips
on a candy cane
around the thought,
so technically you are
"caught" up
in the
midst
of that,
attractiveness

Have you Ever

Have you ever seeked a desire
of something or someone that you admire
that consumed your heart like a burning fire
like the passion to love, & the passion to sing
no matter what it is, passion it bringz
like soft spoken words used for comforting
or a sweet sounding melody
to your ears
that somehow finds it's way into your heart
like a passionate love that bonds together
and never fallz apart

Have you ever
had a love so strong
that you couldn't help but look passed the wrong;
yet you love them
makin aware the difference
between the right & the wrong;
like a simple mistake
the average person seem to make

Have you ever
loved this way

Ephiktion

"Love"
it
should be
"romanic"
it
don't have to be sexual
but yet always
is it to be "ephiktual",
becoming intellectual
enter connecting
the person or people
it's ephikting,
impacting their
mind & body
as a whole
obtaining
the fullness of
their soul
to
caress & console
as in your life
them, do you
hold
in
It

Ephiktion

Expressions

I express myself,
I keep it real,
I tell what it is about you that I feel,
Your beauty,
like a perfume fragrance,
having a strong appeal,
like the unique bottle to the fragrance,
you catch my attention,
but unlike the sweetness of a fragrance held inside
of its bottle,
its like I see it come out
of you;

Its like I see tha thugg aboutcha,
but at tha same time,
I see tha lady come outcha,
like your name,
your are unique,
unlike the earth and its mountain peeks,
you have no boundary
you have no distance to
how far you can reach,
continue to be you,
continue to be unique

Wrong Observation

When you seek
him or her
"them",
"what" do you
"seek"
The
body & booti
or
love & "it's" beauty,
that sex
from a cutie
or
that somethin
"that's" unique

"what" is it that you "seek"

that something that's bleak
that something excit'ing
Like the exploring
of their mind as their
fazique
something that's distinct
"unmistakable"
or
"Is" that what you "seek"

Wrong Observation

Sexxi

Have you ever seen something,
so exquisite,
so unique,
that it's beauty
couldn't be described in no other way,
but
"Sexxi"
like the special relationship
between two; being made one;

Sexxi
like making love,
with soft melodies playing
&
it's midnight,
under the twinkling of the stars
&
glowing of the moonlight
setting the mood
makin everything right
it's
Sexxi

Kissing a body from it's head
down to it's feet,
exploring every each of it's fazique
such as being
on a forever pleasure journey;
"with" the feel of soft lips
gently touching against it's skin

is romantically
Sexxi

Sexxi as
holding close to your touch,
another fazique of bare skin,
feeling it's
warm touch
not only on it's outside
but through to the heart
deep within,
because it's special;

It is
Sexxi

Iz it worth it

Iz it worth it
to be good to some'one
and be treated like "spit"
too get the undeserved
instead of the really needed love,
too be good to them
and you to them don't exist,
but when you don't come around
it's you, they say
they miss;

Iz it worth it,
to you
to be frustrated & depressed
and go through this, you do
"Stop"
evaluate you,
should you continue
to do
the things you do

Iz it worth it
for you
or
Iz it worth it
for them to get all of you
and you nun of them
Iz it Really
Worth "it "

My Desire

Fine like a diamond
beautiful like a butterfly
unique as the smell of a rose,
eyes shining like the stars at night
like something so beautiful
that glow so bright

Warming the coldest place
in a persons heart
some becoming that special part,
the inspiration that the world
fails to desire
the uplifting that the heart require
to be inspired

Unique like a black pearl
like getting married obtaining a wife
no longer being called your girl
entering a different world,
the world of love
something sweet
yet unique
with an endless peek
that life,
is what I seek

So Sad

A love
Once so strong
slowly fading away
becoming weak
&
Broken
the pulling away
of one,
becoming that drive
to push away
the other,
that bond as one
no longer there
&
that love that
was so strong
no longer care,
that instant joy
now
null & void
somethin once joyous
no longer,
is
so;
but
terribly
is,
sadness

Lately its been You

Beautiful as the stars at night
brightening the darkest times in my life,

Sweet as cotton candy
leaving joyful thoughts on my mind
making me happy at all times,

Like a flower that has bloomed,
open hearted & caring
like a guardian angel your always
by my side,

As a teddy bear to a baby
You mean so very much to me

My heart you warm
my journey you seem to end
allowing me to reach
my destiny for love

bringing out the best of me
through love & its beauti

Latey its been you
on my mind

So Many Things
"All about you"

You're my heart
You're my love
You're like an angel from Gods love
Like a Nubian Queen
You're my everything
You're the melody that make my heart sing
You are
the sparkle in my life,
that make me, like a diamond
shine & gleam

You mean so such to me
warming the coolest places in my heart
You're the center of my life
the feeling, that I feel so right

Your
the inspiration, that inspires me,
to keep on keeping on
you're my strength from deep within

My beginning that never end

A Love so Passionate

Beautiful as the changing colors
of fall leaves to the trees,

Like pollinating bees
making thick rich honey,
so shall we be
but making something more thick and lovely

Like shackles to an inmates feet
so shall we be
connected in a way
that no one can separate

But at the same time
to the bond we have
no one can relate
because the seriousness of our connection
is under estimate

That bond and connection
being like a deep passionate affection;

with love being like inmates behind bars
sooner or later to be released;

inside of you burning like a forest fire;
is the love of the hearts desire
Is
A Love so passionate

My Mind

Stuck in My Mind
like candy to a babies fingers
because your so sweet

Running through My Mind,
like a deer in the forest
leaving marks that's permanent

In My Mind like nature existing
always is you,

Like bait to a fish
I'm hooked and I can't let go

Because I'm in love with you
your on My Mind
like the seconds that make time

Like the beat of my heart
that make my blood flow
you are,
the smile on my face
when I'm happy,
you put it there
for the world to stare

Into You

From the essence of your smile
to the grit of your frown, like candy to a child
you drive me wild
Like imprints in, once wet dried cement,
you leave in my heart impressions that are
permanent
cause I'm,
"Into you"
Unlike dirt of clay, these impressions don't wash
away,
leaving with me a constant joy that is pleasing but
like taking a fouler from a baby
can be teasing
So is love
When that love I'm not receiving
yet turned on,
but at the same time,
turned off,
it's like your words, are real, were real,
but what they said was false,
cause you led me on,
presenting something unreal,
which leavez cause to appeal
but yet impression stay
I'm "Into You"
not what you say
because that impressions there,
that you left with, me

Loves Letter

Dear Loveless,
I'm Love
A lot more than sexual
yet simple, emotion filled & effectual,
within you confide I.
Indulgin deep within
caressin your mind
consoling the enters of your being,
of me there's no reason to be scared.
Yeah, I by many am misused, abused, & accused
of "people" having tha blues.
cause "me"
People don't know how to;

Except "me"
Appreciate "me"
& Treat "me"
So "I" Love,
am called a lie, used to destroy,
watch Happi'z soul die.

But "no"
that's not the intension of I
but "is" to fill,
the will of your being,
being something extra special.
Like knowledge intellectual
effectin your persona
with feelins stronger, than sexual

to become in your life
like mandatory labor
your happiness
your keeper.

Askin you is "I" <u>Love</u>
to except me in your "life"
as that wonderful "one"
don't be scared
don't run.
Let me rise within
your soul like the sun
and sits in your heart
as the day is done

Signed
Love

Luv Joy

Pink is the heart
from It's fire of Love,
with a red glow
from its inferno
boiling from below
as Love's magnitude increase
xpressin
joy, happiness, and peace,
revealin all it's best,
and no less
the reality of it's life
constantly confessed,
like bare naked breast
all the way undressed is
Love in it's comfortness,
a sparkling bliss
an exerting excitement not obtained
not content,
yet joyous
xplosive
excited to live
to give to those
that don't have
"its" color of fire
its xpressin inferno
its comfortness
wit bliss,
exerting & xplosive
is
"Luv Joy"

Makin Luv

Somethin special
somethin more than intellectual
yet effectual
beyond a sista or brotha
un'like any otha
deep is love beyond the depths of a canyon
to the point that one can barely
with stand it is love's demand;
'Makin Luv"
creatin something strong
that special somethin to live long
not die young
but to have you like a worn out
spring, "sprung"
continuing to sing the song
you have already sung
creatin a smile so sweet
that the effects of your
presence make the heart skip a beat
the long for that touch
so simple
that smile of happiness
that look of love special
like the treatment of something collectible
a care of somethin extra
more than special
the chemistry in conversation
and the outcome of its creation
is the Makin of Luv in operation

Makin Luv

Unique Beauti

Unlike the shape
of a womens fazique
or
the fine curve
of her booty
cause there's "nothing"
there
but breast at attention
in the air,
So you seek her body
Instead of her,
Instead of
The elegance of her essences
The vibe in her presence
Her character that carry
A distinguished message
Not the stride in her walk
But her character that talk
HER
WHO
SHE IS
HER WAY OF LIFE
Her style of liven
With a soul of given,
Even the shirt off
Her back,
Even though many
would like that;
But to her it's more than that
It's the soft words of conversation

The presence of her smile,
Given off a radiance
Like a strong fragrance

That love of life
Just in the being of its existence;

To the right Person
Given that chance
Too
In her life dance
As deer in the forest
Together
You prance
As she seek to undress
The mind
Of your person
Instead of taken off your
pants

Unique Beauti

Ghyttoetry
(ghetto poetry)

Poetry of life in the hood
and on the streets
that one might be blind to see

-Incarcerated
-On the edge
-Reverse Psychology
-Fam
-Real
-Poetry of the Street
-Thugg Motif
-Juvenile mind
-Listen to the crys
-Unity
-Ghytto Ethycks
-Imitation
-Kon'tamenated
-Locked
-Revoked
-Affiliated
-Rebel rebeller
-Spent
-Walkin with shame
-Spot Light
-A childs Ghytto story

Incarcerated

Locked down in a small space
with nuthin but cold steel
an empty place of lifes lost time
with nothing to do;
but to think,
use time to educate your mind,
thinking on past times, unwind from the bind
that got you so tight and twined,
physically and in the mentally in the mind
Settin lookin at mortar,
cinder blocks and concrete
"nuthin"
but a small empty space a ceil of hell,
that you get to know so well
inside, also near, and around you
inmates you know, don't know,
and don't care to know so you stay to you,
to complete the time that you are required to do
experiencing things not quite right,
so "you" try and keep your surroundings in sight,
prepared to protect yourself and not think twice
as at night you lay your body on
a slate of cold hard steel
and cover your whole body receiving chills
wakin up to a half prepared, unsuitable meal,
that you have know choice but to eat,
to live why am I so mistreated
you say
as you reap the consequences of being
"Incarcerated"

On The Edge

Have you ever been there
like being on the verge of life and death
Like being at the point of having something
at the same time losing it

Have you ever had an aggression to the point of
maintain'in
or snapp'in
like to the point of getting somewhere
and going nowhere
being stuck,
"On The Edge"
between here and there,
in the middle of nowhere

But who cares that your
On The Edge
that you slide down
a razor blade into a alcohol bath
from being
"On The Edge"
like over dosen on drugs
dying or surviving
or
going to rehab to better yourself

On The Edge

Reverse Psychology

Struggle is motivation to prohibit
Hates hesitation in a tryin situation

It is, stimulation for the mind
To establish something divine

Let "it" motivate "your" mind and,
Fall behind, from being blind

Tried by the fires of tribulation
Strengthened like metal elements, by flame

Enduring strength under pressure
To maintain from trials train

Avoid the struggle of strain
&
Obtain tolerance to sustain

Fam

Relatives by blood line
something "everyone" has,
made up of more than "one",
occasionally many members,
but all at the same time
not so close;

All family's not blood related
but will be there for "you"
through the thick & "thin"
from the beginning to the "end"
be there for you
before your blood "kin"

There to make you laugh
comfort you when you cry
keep you alive when you think
your souls about to die;

Gotcha back
"when" you don't got your own
no matter whether your
rich, poor, dirty, or, clean
blue, black, purple, or, green
"ya know what I mean"
"no matter" what the situation

It's love
unlike from above
but its love
cause it's Fam

Real

Real as life and death
real as the empty casing of a spun shell
are the stories that hood tells

Real as a blood spill of someone shot or killed
as real as white chalk body outlines on the pavement

Real as being dead
From a whole through the head
Deadly as dope to a fein
and it's dealers to the streetz
is life on the street

Like the beams of the sun beaten down on the asphalt that make the streets,
burnin the bottom of bare feet

Real like tragedy
as the tone of bricks,
impact'ing your life unexpected, yet very hard
when it hit

and still have to deal with it
not being able to do anything about the unexpected

Poetry of the Street

Wakin in the morning
Lookin upon the hood
Seein a life of turmoil and devastation;

Watchin people live in turmoil
die of devastation,
many struggle but few survive
the drama of the world makes it hard to stay alive
not just physically but mentally

Through a broad vision
you can watch and see
how the bricks & mortar, cement & concrete
is takin control of it's peeps

One at a time
do we watch them fade away
into a place from which it's so hard to escape;

Like entering an abandon building
to make a dope transactions
entering the building with a smile
and dollar signs in the mind,
only to find that they entered the building blind
to loose their money, pride, and, life

Body lyin in a white chalk outline
Loved ones gone
families morn
cause its so hard to let go and move on
knowing that a loved ones gone

Thugg Motif

According to my urban style
and loss fit, baggy dress
my own presentation of fashions stylishness

Categorized by my association with over assertive
ghetto friends
what I do, who I do it with and why I do what I do
to me the title of a thugg has been given

Judged by tha swagga in my walk
the slang in my talk
because you say I'm in places I shouldn't be

Seen as a bad person
because you don't like certain things about me
thought to be dumb because I don't expose
obtained knowledge of
education
Seen to be like everybody and everything but me
who I'm gonna continue to be

Thugg Motif
a portrait painted by society about me
beyond me
cause its not me

Juvenile Mind

Struggles in the house
No love in the home
Turned to the streets
Cause their love is gone

Finding love on the street
They turned to the gangz
Sellin "dope" and doin "violent" things

Dew to the fast transaction of money and having things
Their whole persona of life having changed
They call it makin money so they can eat

But at the same time setup for deceit
In the end what's received?
a life in the penitentiary
a record long as a shirt sleeve

Seein right in the wrong
Love in a negative society
Fastly approaching an ending destiny
To a life in something not to be

Life in a
"Juvenile Mind"

Listen to the Cryz

Listen to the sounds of bullets fly
watch the news see people dying,
then ask yourself the question
"why"
do innocent people have to die,
"Listen"
to the cryz of the ghetto;

Look at life in poverty
no place to lay their head no food to eat,
livin life like nobody on the streetz,
bumbing nickels and dimes
to get something to eat,
"Listen"
to the cryz of the streetz

See how the rich live off of the poor
taking away from them so they can get richer
"Listen"
to the cryz of the economy
Clothes dingy and dirty body smelly from no bath
gritty and grimmy like the streetz
"Listen"
to the cryz of the homeless
"Listen"
to the cryz of the ghetto,
the streetz, the homeless, & economy

"Listen"
to the cryz world

Unity

The togetherness
between
you & me
that make
"we"
"a family"
Like strength in a community
strength in diversity
power in numbers
makin one from many
creatin power by plenty

Unity

Ghytto Ethycks

The hoods right & wrong ways of life,
it's struggle & strive
the tactic to maintain & survive
rules to stay alive

It's presentation of grit and grime,
the hands grind
with life and death on the line

Adapting to the moral conduct
the character and presentation
it present

The ethycks of the ghetto

Ghytto Ethycks

Imitation

As something foreseen to be
Beautiful
Like a seed planted
Not fertilized to grow
Unable to produce like
It's expected too

Like fake plants decorated
From a distance appear to be real
But in it's close up view it's true
Appearance is revealed to be
Imitation

As a person who present their'selves
Like someone their not to be
"please"
Other people
Made to believe something
That's not meant to be

Like bootleg apparel presented as
Authentic
such as fake people actin real

Anybody or anything
Presented or acting
To be what it's not

"Imitation"

Kon'taminated

Like a creek filled "wit" trash
and toxic fluid
killin the "life" that exist within
So does the street and it's
"life of crime"
dead bodies in chalk'd out lines
the polluted minds of the people,
"of the streets"
malignant like spreaded cancer
once minds of the humble & meek
transitioned by the poisons
and venoms of the malice street
Because what wuz searched of
wouldn't found, in the good of people
"trained" to be a man of the "streets"
and wear the crown of a King
&
women wit the royalty of a Queen
or
less,
Livin the lives of thuggz & trickkz
2
rob, loot, steal
or
kill
"havin" no care 4 oth'ers
but
"do" as they feel
Is
"Kon'taminated

Locked

Locked like the natural nappy dreads
twisted
tangled
intertwined
like "2" lovers of "1" mind,
strong
like a hard back books spine
maintainin tha information
held inside
to be confid'ed, with'in
"twistin" your mind to the enters
of its being,
tangled up to the
loosing of your control
for something or someone to grasp and hold
"leavin you"
Locked
In that zone, mind blown gown
like it been hit
by a cyclone,
what you once obtained
no longer do you
Locked
outside of
what you were once "in"
Locked
like the natural nappy dreads
from outside a persons head
Locked

Revoked

Cold as a winter wind chill
frozen "dead" still
a body where no life live
there no soul seem to
exist,

Left face down to
fertilize tha ground
blood spill, gone
dryed up now,

All to be found
is
the remains of a corpse
with an identity
unknown
cause of death
"a mystery"
anotha piece lifes unsolved
history
void;

Gun play,
Death talk,
Bullets fly,

And dead bodies don't "walk"
on the ground they ly

Dope,
Cocaine,
Disease,

People steady dying from the
poison of the street
The asphalt
Holdin the many stains of death
the street lights
seein what the eyez
didn't, catch
with many life's

"Revoked"

Affiliated

A gangstas love,
drugs
tha dope house
tha pen'itentiary
and somewhere in-between somebody
end up dead
the life of a thugg
is that how it begin
&
many times end
a shot out,
drivebye
somebodies gettin popped
anotha dead body
n wit a outline in chalk
constantly
lookin ova ya shoulder
watchin ya back,
hopin ya don't get
caught up,
or
killed
"for dope money"
&
"crack"
So "you" stay
strapped

acquitted
in the waste ban
and on tha hip
claimin
Blood
G
&
Crip
Affiliated
The xcuse
To survive
becoming a way of life

Rebel Rebeller

The Rebel Rebeller
action heller
actions speak louder
than his yell does
they say his words is "not" heard
but his actions are
loud and clear
so clear that you couldn't see,
but hear
the message through,
actions taken
not to be forsaken
like
sex for love makin,
that I don't care love
like a stone wit no feelin
just hard love,
cause that's how it always was

havin a scream louder
than a redneck yeller
Is
The Rebel Rebeller

Spent

Spent,
Is life on the street
like a
merry-go-round
like a
carrousel with lifes
ups & downs'
Is life on unsteady grounds

Spent,
like the revolving chamber of a 38 special
is the request for dope on the street
the constant chase of dirty money

Spent,
like car tires & big wheels
is
the hoods steady rhythm of
lifes being lost, from people killed

"When"

Spent,
should time be to
"unify"
what nigger minded "ignorant" men
designed to diversify
and
weaken
"Soul Unity"

Spent
should be time to
Buildup

The community
Becomez "stronger" in
Unity
Using "diversities"
difference
create positivity

Spent

Walkin with Shame

Like being in jail with cuffs
on the wrist
&
shekels on the feet
in stead of walkin
with a stride
you barely move
your feet
In that jail suit
crossin the street with
your head down
"ashamed" to look around
on the way to the court house,
seen by who you
didn't want to be
left in a state of embarrassment,
walking slow
with your
head hanging low
in that walk of shame
havin possessions of things
you wish you didn't
have to claim
in the midst
of;
Walkin in shame

Spot Lyte

Tha shyne
tha gleam,
tha glamour
tha shame,
all part of the fame
in tha
"Spot Light"

Tha theme
tha reason
of being
in tha spot
of tha light,
tha wrong
tha right,
tha doin of what you like,
tha humble
tha hype
tha lies
tha syke
part of being
in tha light
&
On the spot

"Spot Lyte"

A Childs Ghytto Story

"He say" he's gangsta
"he say" he's a thugg,
from tha streetz he getz love
cause his daddy'z in jail
mama on z
aint no money in tha house
so he had to "mannup"
did what he thought he had
to do
that was called for,

Put a pack on his back
a gun in his hand "now"
he's the man
of the "house"
puttin food in
"they" mouths;
on the grind all night
sleep all day,
should be in school
but in the streetz he play
robbin, stealin, fist fights & gun play
this is the journey of his life every day;

Just 13 ruthless & mean
grimy like the streets
&
no in-between;
Finally daddy write a letter
sayin he'z hearin about him

talkin bout
aint no life in
these cold ass streetz;

but still to survive
"he" walk that unsteady beat,

Meanwhile out tha house "mamazT" turning trickkz
to getta fix
in the process got tha package
and
pregnant,

now stay sick
always in tha clin'ic
but hustling on tha grind
"money"
"he'z" always tryin to "get it"
13 years old but like a man he's livin

A childs ghytto story

Life'oetry
(Life Poetry)

Poetry in the form of lifes realities
hat many may share

- This Life
- Life-N- Brail
- The Antichrist
- M'phasize
- Experience
- Sentenced 2 death
- When we don't understand
- Tyr'd Soul
- Diamond in the ruff
- Graffiti Walls
- Soul Veins
- The Rendering
- Drunk
- Help Needed
- Lookin past the Darkness
- Sold
- To be deceived
- Self Affliction
- Tapped
- Self Xamination
- Feel the Vibes
- Raped
- Naked
- Slow Motion
- Thru tha rain
- Tears in my mind
- Luv Jones
- Xistance
- Seasoned

This Life

Crucial like a twister
crushing houses, breaking limbs
turning cars upside down, leaving people dead

Survivin in this world
seems to be hard as hell
to maintain a positive life
when negative things keep rushing in

Like a killer on the prowl
as a predator to its prey,

that's how it seem when Satans after me
seeking to devour my soul eternally
to establish hell as my destiny

Why do it got to be
that it seems as if
the whole worlds coming down on top of me
in the form of trialz, tribulationz, treacherous'ly

so upon the Lord I call
requesting his majesty
to uplift the burdens of the world up off of me

This Life

Life N Brail

Like feelin for what's not seen
taken a chance with what's unknown
to embrace a new face
life in a new place
feelin for what's "real",
that love you have never had the chance to feel
Life N Brail

Experiencin hell
not seein it before
you go through it
leavin no chance but to do it
no pleasure
but pain
struggle & mental
strain
but hoping in the end that
it's strength you gain
Life N Brail

Like show'n love to someone
and love is not felt
like being dealt a bad hand
and not knowing till the cards
been dealt
is

Life N Brail

The Antichrist

Is it the Antichrist
that tries to persuade the Christian mind
from the way of the divine;

Am I a hypocrite because
I strive to live right, but at times get weak

Was it not the Lord that said;
All have sinned and come short of his glory

Isn't it the Antichrist?
that allow me to struggle, cry out,
and not be heard

Why is it that it seem to be
that the worlds iniquity run free,
and its burden bound me;

Oh tell me, why oh why,
do I get judged so wrongly for what
is right
and the judgment of the wrong seem to be so right

Is it the Antichrist?
that turn heads from the ways of the right
and the vision of the right being blinded with wrong
as right

It is
"The Antichrist"

"M'phasize"

On you
on me
on us as a race
&
community
how we live
what we do
the new clothes,
&
cars
that new pair of shoes;
In your life
cause you got the blues,
put on blast and
made publik nuez
with
"M'phasize"
At the same time,
put in the "dim light"
made not to look so bright
cause shined on
is the negative in our lives
even if we make a change
and do what's right
"cause" we wear nice things
maybe drive something new
it's "something" unkown "neg'ative"
about you
with you
"with"
"M'phasize"

Experience

As a bird in the sky
shot down to die

like a plane
that crash and burn;

Everybody has a turn
to experience and learn,
yearn the worlds sting,
it'z burn
to make a mistake
something everybody tends to make,

Some crash & burn
die or stay alive

Some hold on & be strong
for some their destiny is denied

Some struggle & strive
try to survive
but can't stay alive

Some have no choice but "2" die

The wicked ways of the world
some just can't survive

Sentenced 2 Death

In a life of pain, hell & misery
The existence of what don't
have don't to be
the struggle the strain the refrain
"to maintain"

The hating of me because of who I be,
because of my skin tone
as if I don't exist "like"
I'm dead and gone

Forced to live hard
because of the decisions made by others
that effect "you & me"

Induced like labor into this world
which we must live
but its ways "we"
don't have to be
"part of"
made to make decisions
in which direction we are choos'ing to go

know'ing that these decisions made
can cause us to die early
live life long yet poorly
or
strive to live lavishly
and "loose" your soul
in the midst of it all
you & I
are
Sentenced 2 Death

When We Don't Understand

When trial & tribulation oppress your soul and
physical being,
You want give up and let go
you take it to the Lord and still you struggle
it seems like
to the Lord you have sent
an unanswered call;

But, you don't understand
that the Lord's time controlling,
giving hand, is in the midst
of all the mischief of the world

Why doez it seem that we reap,
what we don't sew
the evil of this world,
leavin the thought in your mind
why is it that these things I go through
Lord what is it with me,
that you tend to do

When we don't understand
That the Lord is a very observing
&
comprehending spirit
that allowz us to endure wisdom
through suffer'ing,
build trust and obtain strength,
be wize "2" obtain knowledge from his ways,
within our soul throughout
to become better beings;

When we don't understand

Tyr'd soul

Worn like an old pair of shoes
drivin hard long miles like car tires
experiencin it's ever existin terraine,
made humble
inflictin "lifes"
war wounds, battle scares, & pains,
not just physically
but deep inside the brain
thoughts train,
a life so hard
it seems impossible to
maintain
is
the Tyr'd Soul
Havin to reach "down"
In the midst of its witts
and be strong like bones
"of"
Calcium
Like grandfather time
In a slow sluggard motion
still pushin on

Tyr'd
Xhausted
&
Dehydrated
Is

"the Tyr'd soul"

Diamonds in Tha Ruff

Isn't it amazing how something
so precious,
can be found in places
so "harsh"
like being held in captivity
for a skill or trade,
worked for less than the
works worth,
because the work produced
is better than expected;

Experiencing the
trial and tribulation
of the world,
Allowing the states of being;
Dazed and confused,
misused and abused,
to be endured
left at the point to which
you don't know what to do,

But through the trials "is"
gained strength
in the form of wisdom,
obtaining the knowledge of
how to use it,
in the form of strength
and
ambition;

Diamonds in tha Ruff

Graffiti Walls

Painted of many colors
expressed through,
thoughts and customs of life as art,
standin out catchin ones "attention"
there everyday
till painted over again & again
then there's still something new to replace it;

Like truth disguised by lies
so can something beautiful be painted over
by something of unwanted presence,

Expressin it's many customs and styles of life
by a viewing, yet unseeing world
not seen for what it is
and
"expresses"
yet showing it's abstract skill of difference

Firm standing & bold
camouflaged with it's unique,
artistic ways,
describing a persons life through authentic art

you, me, we
are
Graffiti Walls

Souls Veins

The enter energy as the drive of ambition
Like perception of intuition leavin an expression
from accomplishing
A mission
As a good harmony of melody makin soulful sounds
musically,
Is soul pumped through the veins like blood to the
brain
Like the rushin force of water that "makes" a creek,
Is the ragin force of enter being,
Inside unseen

Like fertilizer in the soil beneath stimulating the
growth of
What's growin within it
Growin something strong and beautiful outwardly
Growing something wonderful for the whole world
to see
That urge, that drive, that internal motivation,
That provide strengths stimulation;

Souls Veins

The Rendering

Like an animal in a rage
set free giving itself to nature
showing it's presentation through it's
animalistic ways,
using it's animalistic forms
communicating through it's habits
makin known it's presence
is the manner that should be aquired
to be takin with us as being
humanity,
yet trapped inside by deceit
Scared of touchin unknown ground with
sensitive feet,
afraid of presentation in unknown
territory,
mute from the rejection of the world
use to uncorrection like love with no
affection,
not knowing how to except the
positiveness of exception,
with love and affection because it's unexpected,
having it's real presence hidden from
the world like a shy boy or girl,
the tamed character of our humanistic
form of being or creature
We must submit ourselves
to present what we have to offer
with our artistic equaling values
making known to the world what
hasn't been seen

The Rendering

Drunk

Have you ever
had so many things on your mind
that it bringz you
to a stage of "unstability"
"mentally",
to the point
that you may do something
and not realize "it" till after the fact
because your
Drunk
"Not" physically
But "mentally"

Intoxicated off of the negative
things in your life,
your encounter with the world
twistin your mind to the point
that you can't stably think

Cause your

Drunk

What Do You Think

Things I see
things revealed to me
things that shouldn't be
but happen anyway

Should I protest
Should I make a statement
Should I call upon the Lord
makin a request and put it on
the prayer list
or
Should I conceal observation
And digest information
within my brain
and refrain
from the waste of digest'ed
things
or
Should I release myself
Xpressin my feel'ings
as my hummingbird mouth
sings

with it's rough harmony
and uneven melody
sooner or later
somebody's gonna hear me
then heard will I be
till then
I don't know
So

"What do you think"

Help Needed

So many times in life
people miss the key to building
something successfully or positively
you listen to help, to be heard
when you speak
to have the beginning of a never
ending peak
close your mouth open your earz
listen to the worlds cryz
while it shed it's tearz
educate your mind of it fearz
its lionz, tigerz, and bearz,
the thingz of the world
that cause so many scarez
help is wanted
help is needed
its cryz have called
its cryz have pleaded
now attentions to those that'z
calling is needed
cause the minds that make this world
is so conceded
so many times over in this world, is;
Help Needed

When Things Ain't Right

Sometimes I,
walk around with my head hangin down,
can't break a smile,
for a frown,
the wars I fight, struggles,
sometimes seem to get the best of me,
so I go to the Lord
while my heads hangin down and "say"
Lord please bless me,
Strengthen me, and make me strong,
give me the strength, to hold on,
Like a man who receives not love,
but humility,
I'm humble,
Lowly like a homeless man to the street,
God is my strength,
My guidance, that direct me,
he is my up when,
I'm feelin down;
Rich,
unlike man who make the world,
but rich cause I got God,
unlike an impatient man,
I'm meek,
I'm just a simple man,
That none seems to understand,
Yet,
God is the element that makes me,
"who makes me"
who I am,
The existence of my life, that lets me long live

Looking Past the Darkness

When it's seems as if everything's going wrong
Nothings seeming to be right
everything seems to be dark without any
sign of light
but sometimes we have too;
look past the darkness

Lookin to find the least little flicker of light
giving at least a little since of life,
having to look,
and refrain from negative things
to find good in hard times,
and
look past the darkness

In the midst of the darkness
our necks are broken
heads tend to hang down
on our face is nothing but a frown
with our beings crushed, crumbled into pieces
as we attempt too
look past the darkness

On the search for a light that shine bright
instead finding a dim light
giving a sign of hope that everything's
going to be alright
as the pursuit is made

Looking past the darkness
to see the light

Sold

Sold is a story to be told
Leaven no more to unravel, and unfold
Creating a heart to be not hot
but cold

Buying into something that's not so;
but sold

Makin the "sellout" what it is
"because" its sold, its all
leaven itself
with nothing

giving into what should not be,

in that state of fragileness
that state of believing a disbelief
which the disbelief is made too,
be believed

bought into by those, not so wise,
being

Sold

To Be Deceived

Everyday wit the devil,
I dance,
it's like taken a chance with
love & romance,
with his attempt to weaken me
only he strengthens me;

In our eyes what we know as wrong,
he seems to make it feel something like right,
everyday, I see his "mischievous" ways,
disguised in the form of so many things,
something beautiful to deceive me,
in the reflection of his eyes,
I see me
as the prey;
myself for him to slay,
knowing that according to the ways of the world
it's ok,
that's the worlds way, is
to seek out a victim as its prey,
for the slay,
to make it in this world
isn't seen,
but to fail and be deceived
give up, walk away
&
leave
"is" seen,
such as life on the dirty streets,
finding out what you were deceived to see as clean,
to be seen unclean

Self Affliktion

Why do it got to be
that the world is its own enemy,

why are we "our" own enemy
the end to our own "begin'ning",

"we" are the sorrow of our own cryz
that bringz tearz from our own
"eyez"

we sometimez, can be the agony of
"our" destiny
makin thingz what it "don't" got to
"be",
"killing" each other
instead of "loving" one another

Against our own
sistaz & brothaz,
"yet" we say we struggle
"when we" bring "it" to each other,
the battlez we face
the warz we fight
the scarez retained from the
"conflict"
we "afflikt" upon ourselves
"through"

"Self Affliktion"

Tapped

Tapped into Emotions
into unseen feelins
Tapped into something
not seen to be revealed
yet
Like "drill'in" for oil below the surface
not yet knowing of it's existence
until struck
like a nerve under pressure

Tapped
Is a nerve with an
uncomfortable feelin
yet deep
painful
mind chillin
and revealin
leavin the expression
to be show'd
illy

Tapped
into the side of the unseen
the other side of nice
known as mean

From pressure built up
hitt'in deep down below

Tapped

Self Xamination

Why doez it seem that advise that we give
and by many of these things we live,
but to some of our own advise we don't listen
yet when trouble comes and problems occur,
that same advise we wouldn't listen too
now we hear it;

How come as, strong loving
caring beings
we put ourselves in the midst of someone
elses problems seeking to help,
even though their problems begin to get thick
there we still try & stick
although were havin problems worst than theirs

Still we bypass our problems
dealing with theirs
even though all of the time our troubles are
stretching longer
but because we're in the midst of theirs,
we can't deal with our own

Now we need that same strength, love, &, care,
plus more so we can move on

Self Xamination

Feel the Vibes

Throughout me
I try to let
positive vibes thrive
something joyous
something wonderful
that positive side as long as
on this earth I reside

Although in life
suffering & pain I retain
still it's replaced with
something that makes me happy
something that makes me smile
something worth wile

Meanwhile
Even though I smile
it's not always real
as it may appear

I strive for joy to live here
"I say"
let joy reign on me
drowned out dreariness & misery

Like Gods love and,
poetry within me
feel the vibes of positiveness
as they emerge throughout

Feeling the vibes

Raped

Induced
into something beyond willingness
like a women being taken advantage of
sexually
yet unwillingly

getting paid minimum wage
forced to work harder than its worth
to receive a little bit of a "paycheck"
wages deserved not earned

home broken into
things obtained through
hard work
sweat & tears
no longer there

Raped
of what was there
"replaced" wit fear

Raped
Like a bullet gone astray
"t'aken" the life of
something or someone
who it wasn't intend'ed for

The taken of life in which
you never gave existence too

Innocent
&
Raped
of being

"Raped"
Induced like labor
Forced unwillingness
Into a circumstance unwanted

Naked

Like a stripper on a pole
"Xpos'in"
that which was un'xposed

being provoked to tha point of anger
over taken the humble & meekness
revealin the side of the unseen
the dirty & unclean
like the grime washed out of
dirty laundry
is the malice and enmity that's revealed

"Xposin"
things
unknown & unseen
we "all" have a nakedness
about us
whether its there and not
yet revealed
or
its our physical "naked" being
stripped naked we all shall be
oneway
or
another

Slow Motion

In
"Slow Mo'tion"
but moo'vin,
in the territory treaded,
like a farm plow leaven
deep grooves in it,

Not matter'ing
how fast the movement,
but the effects
and
what its do'in,
throughout the territory
on a mission
of prosperity is
the pursu'ant

Pursuing the better of the foreseen best,
being not seen to "do" better
but do "less"

Yet still in Slow Motion go'ing
but slow'ly
not knowing what's before thee
preparing for the futures reality
of what's beyond the knowing to see
while slow'ly moov'ing
in

"Slow Motion"

Thru tha rain

Thru tha rain there'z cryz of tearz
from pain
through these roots its moisture is
obtained

Thru tha rain strengths obtained
fertilized like flowerz made to grow,
nourished from the rain
pumped through the body
like blood through the veinz

Deeply rooted
like an age old tree
to it's "ground"

are you not grow'd
now
from tha rain
which comez down

Thru tha rain
we sometime obtain
strength from pain

if it wasn't for the stormz
and the rain
we would never be
who we be
if we didn't go

"Thru tha Rain"

Luv Jones

Lookin for a love Jones
something other than what
you got a home

a fling
sneek and creep thing

lookin for that
"Luv Jones"
that new feelin
to the bones

Wanna make a new melody
from them new love bones

although what you
got at home,
singz a beautiful song
and shine
like a diamond ring
you still wanna new thing
a
Luv Jones

Sum'thin other than
your own

Xistance

Like being cut
open
by a razor blade
as
words is spilled
from these guts
like blood from the
body
like somebody done
shot me

"So"
shooting back from the mouth
to penetrate the brain
to retain
to replenish
that
which by
the world
is seek'd
to destroy
&
diminish
by evil out of anguish
do these guts speak
a different language
as they are
revealed
spilled

spelling the words of
death
defeat
"killed"
not caring that this vessel
has a
life
meaning
&
will
"to live"
yet into it's Xistance
is delv'd
seeked to end
as
it's guts is spilled
and not
seeked to live

Layin motionless
like death

into this body still
lives life
still breathes
breath

Because in this life
This body
This breath

There is still an
"Xistance"

"Seasoned"

Like a gourmet meal prepared
to culinary perfection
such as pasta to alfredo

So as a person from immature to mature
and the mind from inexperienced to
experienced
as ones life is lived

Properly prepared as roast
with the right
marinades, herb & vegetable
is the mind
when the humble & meek
of one that is tried
with patience & tolerance
is tested

Savoring the mind
with wisdom & knowledge

Makin the character of ones being
more appealing upon it's presence
with appropriate adequates

"Seasoned"
Should we be as a
People
&
Christians

THANK YOU

Personally, I would like to thank the creator of this universe, God the Father for allowing me to live, seeing the day of accomplishment and blessing. Giving a special thanks to Vision Distribution LLC., for working with me and to make putting this book together possible. Also thanking my family, and friends that has supported me throughout this wonderful journey.

                  Sincerely,
                Ricardo A. Owens
                      AKA
                "Sohlja tha Poet"

To Dr Patsey Thomas
Thank you for being that motivation & up lifting spirit

Luv Ya Dearly

Ricardo A Owens

"Sohlja tha poet"

Made in the USA
Charleston, SC
11 May 2010